MATISSE

Published in the United States of America in 1987
by Universe Books
381 Park Avenue South, New York, N.Y. 10016

87 88 89 90 91 / 10 9 8 7 6 5 4 3 2 1

Printed in Italy

Library of Congress Cataloging in Publication Data

Noël, Bernard, 1930—.
Matisse.
(Masters of modern art)
Bibliography: p.
1. Matisse, Henri, 1869-1954—Criticism and interpretation.
I. Title.
N6853.M33N64   1987   709'.2'4   87-13860

ISBN : 0-87663-523-0

Bernard Noël

MATISSE

Translated by Jane Brenton

UNIVERSE BOOKS
New York

Woman Bathing
1909

Everything begins somewhere, and yet there is never a true beginning. What you may identify as a beginning is in fact only a link in a sequence of events, part of a process whose precise origins remain obscure. We may believe we have opened a fresh chapter, but all we have done, essentially, is measure continuity, perpetuating the species, or art itself, or whichever it may be of those eternal verities beside which our efforts dwindle into insignificance.

When Henri Matisse was a young man, Gustave Moreau once said to him: "What you're going to do is simplify painting..." These words marked a kind of beginning, yet the man who spoke them himself embodied a continuity between past and present, and he was looking already to the future. The incident, however, made a deep impression on Matisse; he never forgot Moreau's remark, sometimes recalling it with wry amusement, at other times hailing it as nothing less than a prophetic insight.

On one occasion he described Moreau's reactions more fully: "...'You're not going to simplify painting to that extent, cut it down to that. Why, it would cease to be painting at all'. And then he came back and said: 'Don't take any notice of me. What you are doing is more important than anything I have to say. I'm only a teacher, I don't understand anything...' "

The incident took place at some point between 1895 and 1898, well before Matisse had painted a single picture in the style we regard today as characteristically his. There is an intriguing—and perhaps not accidental—parallel between Moreau's remark and something Matisse himself said much later, in 1942, to the writer Louis Aragon. Contemplating one of his finest pictures, Matisse is said to have exclaimed: "All those years of work, just so that people can say: That's all Matisse is, only that..."

Certainly Matisse thought his comment worthy of being recorded for posterity, since he noted it down in the margin of the manuscript Aragon had submitted to him, a book later published under the title *Matisse en France*, ultimately reissued as *Henri Matisse, roman (Henri Matisse: A Novel)*.

The painter's "only that" refers to the pared-down style foreseen by Gustave Moreau, and at the same time it neatly encapsulates every criticism of modern art ever made. But Matisse, in applying the words to his own work, twists their meaning on its head, so confounding the critics. If "only that " is all they can see, then they are manifestly failing to see the particular "that" which is the painting; it is to their own limited power of observation that the words must be applied. And if they are incapable of distinguishing between the painting itself and their own view of it, how then can they ever hope to see the painter's vision, which is embodied in his painting?

The confusion arises because observation not only supplies information, it also shapes the information it transmits, without however making that distinction explicit. And with Matisse there is an additional source of confusion: he actually capitalizes, in his work, on this peculiarity of observation, transforming the illusory certainty that is our view of the world into a world of his own creation. Painting is a process of revelation; revelation is creation.

Gustave Moreau had a profound influence on a number of painters, among them Rouault and Matisse. He was one of those rare persons capable of teaching, not his own painting (which he was content to practice himself), but painting as such. That was why he encouraged his pupils to visit the Louvre, not so much in order to study the history of art, but to assimilate the essential fact that there can be many different views of the same thing, each a representation reflecting the mind behind it. "I spent my days at the museum," Matisse noted, "and later, as I walked about, I discovered delights comparable to those I had experienced in the paintings."

Moreau painted exclusively from his imagination; Matisse looked instinctively to the outside world; but for both of them the imaginary and the real were no more than the source of motifs. The motif is secondary: it is the material out of which the signs are constructed, a means of expression rather than the expression of a meaning. Moreau and Matisse did not paint the surface of things; they painted the visible layer of appearance imposed on things by observation. If Moreau tends toward exaggeration, it is because he responds to an inner feeling rather than the visible sign; if Matisse tends to simplify, it is because he draws the visible reality into himself and, in and through himself, makes of it a sign.

Moreau's art is visibly complex; Matisse's art is no less complex, but not visibly so: in concealing its origins it also filters out the inessentials. The two painters could hardly be more different, yet it is salutary to remember that they are opposite sides of the same coin: both believe the picture is more important than the subject matter. Both, too, share a belief put into words by Gustave Moreau: "Art is the fevered pursuit by plasticity alone of the expression of inner feeling." And again: "In art, the more elementary the means, the more the sensibility shines through."

The various other influences on Matisse have been discussed elsewhere at such length that it will suffice in this instance merely to list them: Impressionism; Turner (discovered when on honeymoon in London, in 1898); Islamic art (an exhibition at the Musée des Arts décoratifs in 1903); the retrospective of the works of Seurat and van Gogh (1905); the discovery of Japanese prints ("revelation always came to me from the Orient...," Matisse liked to explain); Cézanne ("the Good Lord of painting"). Their effects on Matisse's work are plain to see: rigorous observation, reflected in meticulous construction and freshness of interpretation; mastery of tone and color values—the foundation for composition with color alone; decisive and rapid line-drawing, capable of capturing a subject's essence with insight and subtle simplicity. "I have never avoided being influenced by others," Matisse often emphasized. "I would have considered that cowardice and self-deception."

Matisse was a genius in his handling of both color and construction, and all his efforts were directed to bringing about a union between them—not to making them exist in perfect harmony, which has been achieved by all the

View of Saint-Tropez
1904

great painters, but to rendering them indistinguishable one from the other, something he alone achieved. In letters and in conversation he said again and again, "I always tried to conceal the signs of effort..." In fact he went far beyond that, not only concealing all traces of effort but giving a positive impression of effortless ease, such that the genesis and meaning of the picture are lost in sheer felicity of expression. To the point, indeed, that it becomes almost impossible to say how that felicity was achieved.

Matisse's *œuvre* is unique in its concealment of difficulty, but more than that, it offers absolutely no clues as to the nature of that difficulty. It is as obvious, and as elusive, as reality itself. With other creative artists, whether Mallarmé or James Joyce, Cézanne or Kandinsky or Mondrian, difficulty itself is the route into the work, the key to understanding construction and hence the work itself. But Matisse makes his fellow artists' "difficulty" look like a cheap trick; in his work there is nothing but a seeming simplicity, a seamless surface—unity.

This unity did not simply come into being, spontaneously. Nor is there any easy explanation of it, since it is bound up with the whole history of Matisse's painting, from Fauvism to paper cutouts. Matisse was, *de facto*, a member of the *avant-garde*, although he certainly did not regard himself as such or in any way strive to put himself in that position; nor was he in the least interested in theorizing, although he could on occasion sum up the choices confronting him with great clarity. No one has painted with more deliberation than he, while yet contriving to give the impression of serendipity. Everything in his work is calculated and willed, without in the least appearing to be so. Work is a striving toward liberation; the work of art is not finished until the moment it is set free.

"Unity," of course, ceases to exist the moment you begin to break it down. You can examine its constituent parts. But there a difficulty arises, for you discover that it is not in the construction that the secret lies. "For me, everything is in the conception," said Matisse—revealing all, but explaining nothing. All his pronouncements on art tended to be like this, allusive,

Goldfish
1911

Ivy, Flowers and Fruit
1941

obscure, impossible to pin down to a definite meaning. Usually not about technique at all, but about an attitude, a position taken, an intellectual stance.

Late in his life, in August 1949, Matisse said to Father Couturier: "I am made up of everything I have seen." He might have said exactly that about his painting. In painting, everything he had seen was viewed again through the forms of the everyday environment that provided his motifs—vases, armchairs, and fruit bowls... (for in Matisse's work, the quality of universality is not bestowed on the rare or exotic but attached to the familiar domestic world). The first law of Matisse's universe is that there must always be a subject, but this subject, of necessity figurative, is not the purpose of the picture: its function within the picture is to convey the dimension of universality.

The picture neither describes nor copies its subject; rather it gives it generality, investing it with the significance of "everything I have seen." The most important thing about the subject is that it should reflect what is in the painter's mind; at the same time it should not in any way forfeit its own identity. The challenge the picture offers, its central enigma, is that it may represent a buch of flowers and yet prompt thoughts of something quite different, something not remotely contained within the limits of the subject. "It is in getting into the object that you get inside yourself, "Matisse once said. And "getting into the object" presumably means representing it as it appears to, and is changed by, the artist's perception, and not as it stands there, separate and distinct, before his eyes. The subject licenses the painter to express a train of thought, without ascribing to it a precise and limited significance: the urge is to communicate, not define.

Matisse's history as a painter begins conventionally enough with copies of the old masters: Raphael, Poussin, Carracci, Ruysdael, Chardin, etc. There are also still-lifes putting into practice, with varying degrees of success, the lessons the young painter absorbed from these studies. Matisse said later, to Pierre Courthion, that what interested him about the Dutch painters in

The Dinner Table
1897

particular "was the lightening of tones toward the silvery range... the opportunity to learn how to make the light sing in a muted harmony, to graduate and intensify the tonal range to greatest effect."

The first picture worthy of note—remarkable principally because it marks the end of Matisse's early period—is *The Dinner Table* of 1897. In the corner of a room is a large table covered with a white cloth, set with carafes, glasses, plates, cutlery, fruit bowls, etc; a maid in a white cap and apron is arranging flowers. The overall effect is of a Manet-inspired realism. The reflections and effects of transparency are carefully achieved: it is clear that Matisse wanted to display his skill to the officials of the Salon de la Société Nationale des Beaux-Arts—which he succeeded in doing. What is interesting, in terms of his future development, is the range and brightness of the colors. Also the inclusion of the French windows and two pictures, partly visible, on the walls—elements to which Matisse returned again and again in later paintings.

Just how much this picture belongs with, and sums up, Matisse's early work can be seen from a comparison with *Harmony in Red*, painted in 1908. Between the two a veritable revolution has been effected. In 1897 Matisse was still a painstaking and conscientious painter, trying with little success to open up a restricted volume of space; by 1908 he had achieved the liberation of color and invented plastic space.

Plastic space was the means of creating unity; to the end of his life Matisse was to strive to perfect its use, to make it ever more simplified—and at the same time to conceal unity within that simplicity. The first characteristic of this type of space is that it takes its fundamental structure from the subject, but is not dependent upon it. Thus in *Harmony in Red*, of 1908, we rediscover the table, the carafes, the fruit bowls, and the maid in a white apron, but now they are extras rather than principal actors. The subject no longer governs the disposition of pictorial space: it merely regulates the positioning of the signs, ensuring that their meaning is unmistakable. In *The Dinner Table*, of 1897, space depends in every respect on the subject, to the point where the two seem indissolubly linked; in *Harmony in Red*, of 1908, pictorial space exists in its own right: the subject is still clearly decipherable, but by now even that clarity has come to seem like a distortion of vision. It is evident that there is more to the painting than meets the eye. Resemblance has ceased to be reassuring and begins to raise questions.

Since the Renaissance, all Western figurative painting has, within its system of illusion, treated two different types of representation as one and the same; composition has been used as the means of integrating the one within the other, the representation of the subject within the representation of space, with perspective acting as the means of unifying the two functions, and at the same time ordering what is seen and supplying a conceptual structure. Drawing, self-evidently, has been the basis of this system of representation, it alone being capable of simulating the forms of reality and so providing a basis for the illusion. As for color, it has had little function beyond that of covering the drawing, supplying local color as a lifelike imitation of "real" colors in the real world.

In *Harmony in Red* space itself is red, a rich carmine. This color is not a background; it is, visibly, the air of the picture. The different elements that make up the subject are bathed in this red, just as they would be in the air of the real world. Everything is red: walls and table are what they are only in terms of the way red is given direction by the placing of the blue plant motifs. Everything is red except, in the left-hand corner, the view from the window.

The role played by the plant motifs is paradoxical: their sheer energy and exuberance invite you to believe they inhabit a purely imaginary space: yet their orientation indicates just the opposite, real space. Clearly their function is more than purely decorative, as at first seemed the case: they are designed to point to some fundamental and complex ambiguity within the picture.

Harmony in Red
1908-9

The artificial vegetation of the plant motifs echoes the vegetation, real trees and flowers, seen through the window, and yet the effect of the correspondence is not to emphasize the reality. On the contrary, it is the pure line that is dominant, a line that extends over the surface, holding it together and maintaining an equal intensity over the whole. That line is the arabesque, the flowing curve of which Matisse was to say later, "It is the most synthesizing medium... With a single sign it conveys the totality of things, it makes all sentences into one sentence."

Matisse sought to achieve a mastery that concealed itself. He was one of the great draughtsmen of all time, and yet he sought to eliminate drawing from painting. Claiming he wanted color, and color alone, he nevertheless enlarged the whole notion of what drawing could be. He said once that "drawing proceeds from the spirit"; that it was a matter of "leading colors along the paths of the spirit"; that he had "embarked long ago on a certain shade of ideas"; that he wanted to "inscribe... a spiritual space."

This term "spiritual space" is really no more than another way of designating the plastic space that makes its appearance in Matisse's work around the time of *Harmony in Red*, of 1908. In this context, as a description of space, the meaning of the word "spiritual" should not cause any difficulty. Spiritual space or plastic space is an expressive space, a space impregnated with qualities of the spirit, not fundamentally different from mental space. As such, it cannot be "read" or interpreted, since it is measurable not by its extent or decipherability, but by its visibility. That is to say, by the degree to which it can become visible—which it does by using its ability to unite with the visual powers of the beholder and suborn them for its own purposes.

In his "Notes of a Painter on His Drawing" (1939) Matisse writes: "... my definitive line drawings always have their luminous space and the objects of which they are composed occupy their various planes; they are therefore in perspective, *but in the perspective of feeling...*" This "perspective of feeling" has nothing at all to do with traditional visual perspective; it

Landscape at Collioure :
study for the Joy of Life
1905

Landscape near Toulouse
1898-99

describes an impression that is both felt and seen. Such a perspective is the means of reconciling inner space and outer space, being the unification, in space, of the subject that gives rise to the "feeling" with the "feeling" itself. Matisse goes on to explain that, for him, drawing is "a medium for the expression of inner feelings and the description of moods." By this he means that a drawing, in appearance a simple rendering of a subject, is in fact a projection of inner feeling, realized with the assistance of a subject. Later, having explained that he does not like the word "mood," he writes that the "emotional impact" his models have on him "is not especially apparent in the representation of their bodies, but often in certain lines or values that extend over the whole of the canvas or paper and supply its orchestration, its architecture. Although not everybody notices this. It is perhaps a sublimated pleasure..."

Orchestration, architecture, sublimated pleasure—these are the terms he chooses to describe the attributes and functions of expressive space. What is remarkable is that none of them refers to a visual response—proof, if it were needed, that plastic space, as conceived of by Matisse, does not appeal to the visual senses except as a means of arousing "feeling."

Matisse simplifies his painting to make it express the essential in himself. He said to Aragon: "Make no mistake: I am not saying that I see a tree out of the window and I try to copy it. The tree is also an amalgam of the various effects it produces in me. It is simply not a question of drawing the tree that I see."

Apparently, the point is not to draw "the tree that I see" but "the tree that I feel." But in what way are they different? The former is situated in visual space, the latter in expressive space, which includes "what I see" within the totality of "what I feel," subsuming the outer world within the inner world, or vice versa. It is the same mechanism as the painter uses to make visible something that itself is not visible. "Feeling" is always rooted in a subject that is visible and capable of being represented, yet it operates within an invisible inner sphere of reality. Hence the fact that in Matisse's works there

Notre-Dame in the Late Afternoon
1902

must always be a figurative subject existing in an abstract space. This conjunction of identifiable figure and abstract space is indeed what characterizes Matisse, and it is also the reason why the "difficulty" of his work is so hard to pin down, for the abstract element is always disguised, appearing perhaps as the representation of pictures within pictures, or suggested only by the simplification of the pictorial scheme.

The transition from traditional space to abstract plastic space is linked in Matisse's *œuvre* with the move to pure color in the period 1898-1900. Perhaps pure color is itself the highest form of abstraction? Its pretext is representation, but its true justification is sheer pleasure, and an intensity quite beyond the purposes of representation. It is not hard to see why pure color took such a hold on the painters of the time, leading to the emergence of the Fauves in 1905. It should be said, however, that they made the mistake of confusing intensity with excess and, with the sole exception of Matisse, rapidly reverted to using color in a traditional way.

Pure color was a revelation to Matisse. It was one of those moments in history when an individual is perfectly in tune with his time, both the product of his age and the right man to act as its interpreter. Following on from the Impressionists and Toulouse-Lautrec, van Gogh, and Gauguin, it was in a sense inevitable that color would come to be used as Matisse used it. In fact, one can trace the roots of the phenomenon back even further. There are intimations already in the zones of pure color ventured on occasion by Ingres, in some of David's more spontaneous backgrounds, in Delacroix's and Girodet's frenzies of color, in the spectacular effects of John Martin and the landscapes of pure color by Caspar David Friedrich, such as *Monk on the Seashore* or *La Grande Réserve*. Also, and preeminently, in Turner, quite simply a painter before his time.

Matisse often discussed color, but always in relation to his own usage, and to "feeling," not in terms of theory or historical usage. For example, he said once, "Colors have in themselves, independently of the objects they serve to express, a significant influence on the feelings of whoever beholds them." And again: "Fauvism happened because we moved right away from colors of imitation, and because with pure colors we obtained stronger reactions, much more marked simultaneous reactions; and then too there was the luminosity of the colors."

As early as 1898 there are instances of "luminosity" in Matisse's work, in for example *Landscape near Toulouse*; "strong reactions" are the most striking feature of *Notre-Dame in the Late Afternoon*, of 1902, where the whole space is lit and structured by broad expanses of color that can by no stretch of the imagination be described as the color "of imitation." A decisive step was taken in the summer of 1904, when Matisse joined Signac at Saint-Tropez. Signac was not only a close friend of Seurat, he was also the theorist of the Divisionists. Matisse experimented with some of their ideas and, back in Paris, tried them out in a large canvas entitled *Luxe, calme et volupté*, which aroused much comment at the Salon des Indépendants of 1905. The painting is oversystematic and rather stilted; yet the process of methodically juxtaposing rectangular brushmarks over the surface did at least rid Matisse of any last urge to resort to mechanical formulas, and the pursuit of "luminosity" was the means of his liberation from academic conventions of realism. If Matisse was capable of transcending both tradition and modernism, it was because he approached them experimentally and did not elevate them to the level of dogmatic certainties.

By the following summer, when he stayed in Collioure with Derain, Matisse had already rid himself of all the trappings of Divisionism. But he had learned from it one lesson. Instead of covering the surface with tiny dots and rectangles, he now applied a series of bold, expansive brushmarks, which indicated the forms and yet at the same time retained their identity as distinct and separate visual units. On occasion the marks lengthened and became lines, or they spread out into zones of color, but always it was pure color, stretching, pulling, and expanding in all directions, emerald greens, vermilions, and cobalt blues, their violence and crudeness tempered to a vivid spontaneity by the interpolation of other pure colors softer and lighter in tone, mauves, yellows, and pinks.

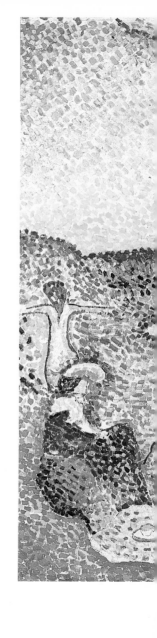

Luxe, calme et volupté
1904

The Joy of Life
1906

Madame Matisse
or The Green Line
1905

The Young Sailor II
1907

Marguerite Reading
1906

Algerian Woman
1909

It was also in Collioure that Matisse discovered the luminosity of black. The story was passed on by Raoul Dufy to Matisse's first biographer, Raymond Escholier: "Things were not working out as he wanted. He could not achieve the amazing brilliance of the Mediterranean light, when suddenly, breaking with all the Impressionist theories, he seized a tube of black and forcefully outlined the window frame. That was the day when, out of black, he created light."

Over the next few years Matisse produced the string of masterpieces that made him beyond question the dominant figure of the Fauve group: *The Open Window*, 1905; *Landscape at Collioure*, 1905; *Siesta*, 1905; *Woman with the Hat*, 1905; *The Green Line*, 1905; *The Joy of Life*, 1905-6; *Marguerite Reading*, 1906; *Marguerite*, 1907; *The Young Sailor II*, 1907; *Boy with Butterfly Net*, 1907; *Woman Combing Hair*, 1907; *The Game of Bowls*, 1907; *The River Bank*, 1907; *The Algerian Woman*, 1909; *Woman in Green*, 1909; *Girl with Black Cat*, 1910.

Fauvism was not a school of painting; it was more a fortuitous encounter. At the Salon d'Automne of 1905, the works of Matisse, Camoin, Derain, Friesz, Manguin, Marquet, Puy, Rouault, Valtat, and Vlaminck were hung together in Room VII, the central area. It was a hanging scheme designed to show off their similar use of pure color, and the impact was electrifying. A critic called Vauxcelles was so outraged by the violence of the raw color that he described a Florentine sculpture in Room VII as being like a "Donatello surrounded by wild beasts" *(Donatello au milieu des fauves)*. It was the last word *fauves* that was taken up and gained currency, becoming the label of a movement that had not hitherto existed in any real sense, the painters in question having been united by little more than friendship and affinity.

Matisse was a Fauve because he was Matisse, not because he aligned himself with any preexisting theory of painting. Fauvism was no more than an episode in his life, although certainly the controversy it aroused did not hinder his growing reputation. He had his first one-man show at Vollard's in

Le Luxe I
1907

1904, and he was beginning to sell to collectors—notably, from 1905 onward, to Leo Stein, brother of the famous Gertrude. As a result, Matisse was in a secure position to plan and execute the large compositions that followed *The Joy of Life: Le Luxe I*, 1907, and *Le Luxe II*, 1907-8, and also two commissions from the Moscow collector Sergei Shchukin, *La Danse* and *La Musique*, 1910. The conception of color is the same here as in the series of pictures listed above, although a growing importance is attached to outline and flat color, reflecting Matisse's drive toward simplification. He declared at the time, to Estienne: "We approach serenity through the simplification of ideas and of the plastic. Wholeness is our only ideal..."

Evidently "wholeness" is synonymous with "unity," the synthesis of the felt and the seen. In *La Danse* and *La Musique* simplification is carried to extremes: there are just three colors and five figures. Never before had Matisse succeeded in being so concise, and his success is the more impressive when one considers the difficulties of achieving pure expression without lapsing into symbolism. Matisse chose his three colors: "a beautiful blue for the sky, the most beautiful of blues (the surface being saturated with pigment, that is, saturated to the point where blue, the idea of absolute blueness, is fully realized), the green of the hill, and the vibrant vermilion of the bodies. With these three colors I had my luminous harmony, and also chromatic purity—the sign this was so being that the form altered according to the way the juxtaposed colors reacted together. For expression comes with the beholder's apprehension of the colored surface as a whole."

The last sentence sums up Matisse's goal of "expression" as a product of "wholeness." For this to be achieved, it is necessary first to replace "feeling" itself with the *concept* of "feeling," in order that its "perspective" may be introduced into a composition capable of stirring the beholder by its "wholeness"—a wholeness consisting not merely in the totality of the elements on the canvas but also embracing the beholder's act of seeing. We are dealing here not with compositional unity in the classic sense of the term, but with the power of such a composition to unite the work of art with the observation of it. The distinction between the "perspective of feeling" and traditional perspective is thus clarified. Perspective introduces into vision an abstract organization, so that we accept the concept of reality as representing reality itself, and do not distinguish between the two. The perspective of feeling acts in the opposite way: It does not trick vision into seeing a semblance of realism, instead it enhances and restores emotional intensity, making a space that is communicative in its effects. Chromatic purity was the key to the discovery of this quality of space. As painters moved away from pseudorealistic local color they experienced the liberation of expressive color—which, devoid of specific content, offers no clues to the beholder who is not prepared to open his mind to new experience.

In the most important of his published writings, "Notes of a Painter," published in *La Grande Revue* of 25 December 1908, Matisse explained: "What I strive for above all is expression... Expression, for me, does not consist in passion breaking out on a face or making itself felt in a violent gesture. It lies in the whole disposition of the picture: the area occupied by the bodies, the empty spaces around them, the proportions, everything has its part to play. Composition is the art of arranging in a decorative fashion the various elements the painter has at his disposal to express his feelings. In a picture, each part will be visible and will play the role appropriate to it, primary or secondary. Everything that is not of use in the picture is, by that token, detrimental to it. A work of art must be a harmonious whole: any superfluous detail would take the place of some other essential detail in the mind of the beholder."

In this passage Matisse rejects just those outbursts of passion and violent gestures that have always provided the "expressive" content of classical and Romantic painting, and which, carried to extremes, are characteristic of Expressionism. Clearly, it is impossible to regard Matisse as an Expressionist, even though other aspects of his work would tend to identify him with the movement. And, equally, it is impossible to define precisely the nature of this "expression" that Matisse "strives for above all." We know it is an effect produced by the picture as a whole—an effect that is visual and

Top :
La Musique
1910

Bottom :
La Danse
1910

Prepatory study for La Musique
1907

Window at Tangier
1912

French Window at Collioure
1914

yet invisible, because it is apprehended by "feeling." Although "each part" is "visible," the painter constructs a "whole" which is "expression" and which—even though it operates only through vision—does not reach its full intensity until it penetrates beyond retinal vision. To what insubstantial or mental realm Matisse does not say, but he declares, again in the "Notes": "I want to achieve that distillation of the feelings that makes the picture. I could content myself with a work excecuted spontaneously, but later I would tire of it, so I prefer to keep reworking in order that later I can see in it a representation of my own mind..."

Successful "expression" thus transmits "that distillation of the feelings," but Matisse does not recognize it as being successful unless he sees in it "a representation of my own mind." In other words, all "expression" is a channeling of the feelings, starting with an inner experience, and leading, at its destination, to the release of a comparable experience. What is mysterious about "expression" is that it is created and transmitted through vision, yet it uses the visual as a means and not as an end. The more you study it, the more clear it becomes that "expression" does indeed function as a channel of communication between internal and external space, via the space occupied by the work of art.

Visual expression cannot satisfactorily be rendered as a written expression. The former has an immediate synthetic impact; the latter does not. In a visual statement everything is focused and distilled in advance, while a written statement is discursive—it is, if you like, a continuous process of distillation. How then could we even begin to describe, for example, the expressive content of *La Danse?* Looking back to the series of major compositions that followed *Luxe, calme et volupté*, there is one title that may provide a key: *The Joy of Life*.

Perhaps in itself the phrase means nothing very much. But if you look at the implications behind the words, then they begin to make a sort of sense.

In "Notes of a Painter" Matisse wrote: "What I dream of is an art of

Notre-Dame
1914

equilibrium, purity, and tranquillity, devoid of upsetting or troubling subject matter, which could serve for anyone who works with his brain, whether for example a businessman or a man of letters, as a balm, a soothing influence on the mind, something like a good armchair that provides relief from bodily fatigue."

And that is as far as Matisse will go; he will not admit to having any ambition beyond beauty and tranquillity, delight and perfection, not even if it means hearing himself say, "That's all Matisse is, only that." It is a fact that you can look at any painting by Matisse and experience simple pleasure, or "joy," for it will be full of visual delights. No explanations seem to be required since the painting looks perfectly straightforward. The paradox with Matisse is that this immediacy is achieved through the exercise of consummate skill. If you study his work you can see the thought that went into it, but if you simply look at it, all that is forgotten. Indeed the more you study Matisse, the more you realize that Matisse intended you to forget.

In order to confer that liberation of forgetting on the beholder, Matisse himself had not only to solve the problems but also to provide a solution that left no evidence of difficulty existing in the first place: it was a process that was of a piece with his desire to make painting a "soothing influence on the mind," even though it was created out of hard deliberation and intensity of "feeling." Emotional responses are not all exalted and dramatic; there can be quiet contentment and happiness as well as ecstasy. Has it not after all been the goal of every society to achieve such happiness—precisely that "joy of life" Matisse reflected in his paintings? Although Matisse went beyond outward appearances, he painted the expression of happiness itself, as something that is within ourselves, not in some far distant paradise, something he himself experienced and was able to externalize in work. "It is a question," he wrote, "of channeling the beholder's mind in such a way that he relates to the picture but is able to conceive of something quite different from the particular object we chose to paint: a question of holding his interest without tying him down, inducing him to experience the quality of the feeling expressed."

The years 1911 to 1917 were dominated, for Matisse, by the attempt to rationalize the processes of simplification, and then to transform intellectual effort into "serenity." As a painter, he had already experienced the liberation of pure color; now, as a draughtsman, he found liberation in linearity, conferring on line the ability to take its place in both signs and figures, in space and in form.

The first picture that betrays these preoccupations is *The Conversation*, of 1911. A number of elements are set in a blue space: to the right, a woman in a black dress with green at the neck; in the center, a window; on the left, a man, standing. The woman is seated in an armchair, blue like the blue space, suggested by a few lines. The window is merely an opening, with no indication of glass panes or uprights; the wrought-iron balustrade stands out against it as a sharp black design. Framed in the window aperture, ranked one above the other, are a patch of green grass, a tree, three blue masses with red flowers and, at the very top, a window with panes of blue glass. The man standing on the left wears a striped jacket and trousers (perhaps pajamas), emphasizing his verticality; the beard suggest that this may be a self-portrait. The man and woman face each other, in profile, the open window between them.

The conversation takes place within a single flat plane, corresponding to that of the characters' profiles. The plane that corresponds to the window aperture, although it lacks perspective, is lit in such a way as to suggest space. We see the man's right eye and the woman's left. The two eyes look straight at each other and could represent the two ends of a line—which is, however, as invisible as the painted conversation is silent. The line joining the eyes may be seen as one side of a triangle, the base of which is formed by the figure of the man; the remaining side of the triangle runs through the woman's right hand to the bottom of the man's legs. And it would be perfectly possible to go on to analyze the "triangle of the conversation" still further, examining the relative positions of the different parts of the two bodies. The woman's décolleté also forms a triangle, set within the triangle of her green collar; there is a further triangle linking the three light patches of her face and hands...

The Conversation
1911

The figures look at each other across the pictorial space, and that space is flat, absolutely flat, in a way that first surprises and then unsettles the beholder. Even the plane of the window aperture, invitingly perpendicular to that of the conversation, proves to lead nowhere. All we are offered is a painted image, in which there is nothing that is not contained. Here we have the first example of Matisse's concise style, what he described to Louis Aragon as "only that"; the picture represents, quite baldly, a look being exchanged between two people, laid out as a flat image—and yet, flattened as it is into a single plane, that look is meaningful in a way that makes the picture acquire a depth of another kind, a depth, if you like, of significance. In this pared-down world, it is the limitation of each element that is important: the painting is indeed a channeling of experience, but the route through is blocked. The only way to proceed is via oneself; it is a predicament echoing that of Matisse himself, as the painter of the picture—and as a painted image within it.

It was in the same year, 1911, that Matisse painted *Goldfish; The Blue Window; Interior with Eggplants; The Pink Studio;* and *The Red Studio*. Each of these masterpieces treats the visible space in a different way: in *The Blue Window*, for example, by structuring its insubstantiality, while still allowing it to play freely over the objects; in *Goldfish*, by literally containing it, and then placing the other elements concentrically all around. The most striking feature of the three large interiors is the way they invoke a number of different spaces within the larger space, either by including pictures within the picture, or by showing the view seen through a window, or in a mirror. Where there are pictures, these are always by Matisse himself, and therefore represent the past tense of the present picture; at the same time they suggest continuity. They are like false windows, which open onto a view supplied by the painter; the true windows, on the other hand, are like false pictures; and they too open onto nothing more than a view supplied by the painter. The mirrors serve to bring into view something that could not otherwise be seen, and they allow the painter to introduce himself into the picture.

"An artist," said Matisse, "should be aware when he reasons that his

The Pink Studio
1911

Large Interior with Eggplants
1911

picture is a fiction, but when he paints he should have the feeling he has held a up mirror to nature. And even when he has deliberately avoided doing that, he should be convinced it was only in order to render it more completely." Painting, in other words, is only painting, but what the painter creates out of it goes far beyond "only that." He is like one of the old icon-painters: if his image is true, its truth will shine out and be communicated.

The desire to create these channels, or pathways, led Matisse to "architecturalize" the field of view, at first breaking up the surface with crude triangulations, but later producing a number of paintings of a sublime harmony, among them *Marguerite, Head White and Rose*, 1914, and *View of Notre-Dame*, 1914. The composition of *French Window at Collioure*, 1914, with its broad vertical planes framing a black aperture, seems to echo the architecture of the real world. Pure black is used here to represent light, as it is too in three other major pictures: *The Gourds*. 1915-16; *The Moroccans*, 1916; and *Bathers by the River*, 1916. Writing of *The Gourds*, Matisse appears to have forgotten his first use of the color in this way—on the occasion recalled by Dufy: "It was in this picture that I began to use pure black as a color of light and not a color of darkness." And, once again, he explains to Tériade: "My picture *The Moroccans* represents the beginning of expressing myself through the color, through blacks and their contrasts." Pure black is also a significant element in *Lorette with a Green Dress, Black Background*, 1916, and *The Painter and His Model*, 1917.

In this latter picture the central figure is a painter, seated on a chair. His face is not visible, because he is at an angle: all we can see are his left cheek and the nape of his neck. He is probably looking at the canvas on the easel or at the model clad in a green dressing gown, who occupies a mauve armchair. To the painter's right is a window. This arrangement means that model, picture, painter, and window occupy the four points of a diamond, which breaks up the picture surface—as too does the dark vertical strip which runs into the dark portion of the floor, contrasting with the light strip of floor which runs into the light surface of the wall. In the area of light are the easel and the outline of the armchair; in the dark area is the painter, but the

The Piano Lesson
1916

Violonist at the Window
1917-18

The Painter and His Model
1917

picture on the easel serves to bring an element of darkness into the light... There are three heads, two of them real, belonging to the painter and the model, and one unreal, an element in the picture on the easel. In practice, of course, all three are unreal, since all three are painted—although there are, perhaps, degrees of reality. The picture within the picture is set against a dark ground. Perhaps this reversal is intended to emphasize that reality is more intensely itself *in its image*, that it then becomes an "icon" of itself, a supremely powerful presence? The picture on its easel faces the open window, just as the world of ideas stands in relation to the real world... The three heads mark out the picture's "center," a taut volume in which the model and her double are set in confrontation beneath the empty regard of a large baroque mirror, itself in the shape of a diamond...

The expressive tension creates a depth in the flat surface, so that the eye is invited to progress into the picture. It is a visual experience of a very different kind from that of surveying the smoothly integrated planes of *The Piano Lesson*, of 1916, another major picture of the period. In the one picture the senses are invited to engage with the *expressive* content; in the other there is a pleasurable gliding from surface to surface, a sheer delight in the way everything falls harmoniously into place.

In 1917 Matisse moved to Nice: "work and sheer joy" was how he later described his time there. This was the period of his odalisques, interiors with slatted shutters, carpets, divans, draperies, and nudes. The arabesque was the hidden motif, indeed often the only motif licensing the extravaganza of red, blue, lemon yellow, black, vermilion, mauve, and pink. It was a feast for the eyes, a celebration of the visual world. "For me," Matisse wrote to Raymond Escholier, "nature is always present. It's the same as being in love; everything hinges on what the artist unconsciously projects onto what he sees. It is the quality of that projection that imparts life, much more than the presence before the artist's eyes of a particular living being."

The "joy of life" is a choice. It reflects a particular attitude of mind. Through color, Matisse discovered his means of "expression." Color *was*

Odalisque with Red Trousers
1921

Odalisque with Magnolias
1924

Odalisque with a Moorish Chair
1928

Seated Nude
1930

space, not used realistically, but never apart from the figures. A tapestry, a bunch of flowers, a face, were simply there, *in* the color, just as "feeling" was in the eye of the beholder.

The problem with such a picture is that it is redolent with significance, and yet it does not mean precisely one thing or another. Matisse said frequently that painting for him was "ordering the brain," he was aiming to replace "explicatory detail with a living and evocative synthesis." And expression that is evocative and allusive is fundamentally different from expression that is explanatory and explicit. You cannot simply assimilate it and pass on. Its effects are lingering.

"Mastery of one's craft," said Matisse, "should pass from the conscious to the unconscious, only then does one succeed in giving that impression of spontaneity." You are immediately reminded of the wonderful freedom of *Odalisque with Red Trousers*, 1921, or *Decorative Figure on an Ornamental Background*, 1925-26—but it is important to remember that Matisse's "spontaneity" is in fact a manifestation of patient and self-effacing skill of the very highest order.

The late twenties saw the beginning of a new period of work. It started with a journey and a commission. The journey took Matisse to Tahiti, via New York, Los Angeles, and San Francisco: "It was only the light that interested me," Matisse was later to say. He seized eagerly the opportunity to explore all the different qualities, the different vintages of light; we know, for example, that he particularly relished the "crystalline" atmosphere of New York, preferring it to the golden glow of the Tropics. Light enriched his creativity—although its influence was not immediately reflected in his work: being Matisse, he needed time to assimilate what he had seen into his mental life. Experience had to be distilled by memory.

The commission came from one of Matisse's American collectors, Dr. Albert C. Barnes, who required a large decorative piece—52 square meters in area—for the large vaulted hall he had recently had installed as a private museum. The commission posed a number of complex problems

The Dream
1935

Woman with Blouse, Dreaming
1936

The Romanian Blouse
1940

because of the peculiar constraints of the space to be decorated, consisting of three semicircular lunettes linked by a long horizontal panel but separated from each other by the lower extensions of the roof arches.

Matisse was to work for almost three years (1931-33) on a new interpretation of a dance theme, known as the Merion *Dance*, after the place where Dr. Barnes lived in the USA; a first version could not be installed because the original measurements were inaccurate, and that is now in the Musée d'Art Moderne de la Ville de Paris. In the Paris version there are six figures, in the Merion version, eight. The rhythm of the composition derives out of the movement to the bodies, but that movement flows entirely from the calligraphy of the contours—color being expressed simply as zones of flat, uniform color: light gray for the dancers and black, blue, and pink for the strips of background.

Matisse did not work from a small-scale model but launched straightaway on the full-size design, using for the first time cutout papers which could be fixed to the wall and then rearranged. Since he believed that "the composition... changes according to the surface to which it is applied," it was out of the question for him to work on a maquette and then simply enlarge it to create the final version. That decision is highly significant, proving that, for Matisse, there was an inescapable link between the conception of a work and the size of the space it was to occupy—a link between quality of creativity and scale. Space could not become expressive space unless the proportions were respected: "... if the relationships are to come alive," Matisse said, "all the precise dimensions must actually be experienced."

Never before had Matisse achieved such economy of line, creating line out of color itself and not through drawing. And it was this realization of a simultaneity of line and color that made possible an even greater simplification of the figures in the pictures that were to follow—a transition, indeed, from form to sign. Paradoxically, however, the sign as used by Matisse does not imply abstraction, but rather the concretization of something that is present.

One could if one wished compile a sort of inventory of the signs used by a particular painter, but since each sign is meaningful only in the context of the specific picture, such an inventory would not supply even a basic key to meaning. It is simply not possible to transfer the significance of one picture to another: If the same sign is used in a different picture, it becomes a different sign. Matisse worked all his life with what Aragon called "a palette of objects": vases, fruit bowls, armchairs, etc. Yet any attempt to define and classify these objects, any attempt to trace their usage, is bound to be fruitless, unless perhaps in identifying a general theme. You cannot ascribe a fixed meaning to the object. You must simply be prepared to look each time at what is presented, respond with the feelings, and proceed from there...

Take, for example, *Pink Nude*, 1935 ; *The Dream*, 1935 ; *The Persian Robe*, 1937; *The Romanian Blouse*, 1940; *Still-life with Magnolias*, 1941. We know that Matisse spent nine and six months respectively working on the two latter pictures. We know that because, for once, he intended us to understand the price of simplicity. A red background, a blue skirt, a white blouse with a pattern of repeated motifs... If this were an abstract painting we would respond to its rhythms and there would be no problem. The confusion arises because it is a figure that is simplified in this way—and we easily forget that any attempt to express anything at all demands a kind of abstraction, a compression of meaning. Plastic expression, as Matisse conceived of it, involves an interaction between conception and feeling: "I work from feeling. I have the conception in my head and I try to realize it. Very often I may change my conception... But I know what I am aiming for..."

We may imagine the painter's "feeling" as a space that he is slowly exploring; and the painter's head, in the middle of this space, like a dial, set fixed to the due north of the picture's conception. The process continues for some time: the exploration of feeling, with the head acting as a guide, saying when to hold back and when to go forward... Until, eventually, the face of the dial and the space of feeling—or, equally, the surface of the canvas and

Woman Reading,
Black Background
1939

Woman on a Sofa
1920-22

The Egyptian Curtain
1948

The Persian Robe
1937

the mental compass of the head—have come together and are congruent, indistinguishable. Only then is the process is complete.

The Romanian Blouse is probably the painting that best illustrates Matisse's patient method of exploration, since we know the picture took nine months to complete, and there is even documentary evidence of its gestation: the series of photographs Matisse had taken of each successive state before overpainting it. The painting is widely cited by the critics as demonstrating the difficulty inherent in achieving simplicity (which, of course, is just another way of describing what Matisse ironically referred to as "only that").

The painting's immediacy is undeniable. It is a "whole," and if you dwell on the details you lose sight of that whole. What does Matisse mean when he discusses the relationship between "feeling" and "conception"? That the painter is expressing something that has been first conceived in the mind, but, since painting itself is not conceptual, he must work "from feeling"; and so, through feeling, realize his conception—make it felt, and thus intelligible.

Matisse realizes his conception by working from a model. The traces of the work are hidden but the model remains, so the model becomes the figure of his expression: it becomes, in fact, a sign. It is a sign, even, of dual significance, since it represents both feeling and conception, relating both to the person who is posing and to the painter observing that person. Plastic expression is the means of making this relationship manifest within one figure and in a single space.

The continuing presence of the object or the model serves, in a sense, as the affirmation of its necessity. The paradox of a picture like *The Romanian Blouse*—and it is also a risk, willingly taken—is that its unvarnished simplicity may be interpreted as anecdotal as well as expressive. It was precisely to free himself from the trap of particularity that Matisse used a model or a "palette of objects." In 1942 he said to Aragon: "For others the

Dancer and Armchair,
Black Background
1942

model is information... For me it is something that draws my attention... it is the focus of my energies." And on another occasion: "You understand, I paint thought objects by plastic means: if I close my eyes I see the objects better than with my eyes open, stripped of all their little peculiarities, and it is that which I paint."

As early as 1908, Sarah Stein noted down Matisse's advice to his students: "When you confront the subject, you should forget all your theories and ideas. That part of them that truly matters to you will reemerge in the expression of the emotion awakened in you by the subject."

In 1909, Matisse said to Estienne: "I'm going to paint a woman's body; first I think hard about the form... What I am doing is distilling the meaning of that body."

In 1925, to Jacques Guenne: "... the secret of my art. It consists in a meditation on a theme from nature."

In 1930, to Tériade: "My work duplicates my mental life." And he went on to say: "Most painters need a direct contact with objects in order to feel they exist, and they cannot reproduce them except under these strict physical conditions. They seek an external light to provide their own illumination. The artist or poet, on the other hand, possesses an internal light that transforms objects, and makes of them a new world, a world that can be experienced, a world that is coherent and alive—which is the infallible sign of divinity, the operations of divinity."

In 1935, in *The Studio*, no. IX: "A picture is the coordination of controlled rhythms... I decided then to put aside any concern for verisimilitude. Copying a subject was of no interest to me. What advantage was there in copying a subject that nature supplies in unlimited quantities, and that you always feel could be improved upon. What matters is the relationship the object has to the artist, and to his personality, and the power it has to give coherence to his sensations and emotions."

Hélène
1936

The Inhabited Silence of Houses
1947

Yellow and Blue Interior
1946

Primavera
1938

The consistency and clarity of Matisse's position notwithstanding, there remains a paradox, what Aragon called "one of the great Matisse mysteries": that "on the one hand Matisse cannot dispense with a model, and on the other hand the model inspires him to produce something of such freedom."

Aragon presents quite brilliantly the "drama of the model," using a number of photographs of the "palette of objects" (rococo armchair, Louis XV chairs, "old chairs," pots, fruit bowls, milk-glass, cut-glass, sweet jars, etc.) in conjunction with a series of photographs showing Matisse at work with his model, a dark-skinned young woman. It is a brilliant montage, and yet the central mystery remains, unresolved. The physical representation of the objects used by Matisse sheds no more light than a verbal recital of the figures contained within a picture.

For the "drama" is not physically enacted, it is not visible, but a drama of the mind: it lasts only as long as the painter projects onto the model a mental quality, which does not become visible except as it is reflected on the paper. The model acts as a mirror for the painter's thoughts; it is, however, an active mirror—it forces the painter to work at the reflection until it merges perfectly with the image of the object in which it is reflected. Thus there is an interplay of surface image and reflection—not so much a drama, you may say, as a comedy of mistaken identity. Matisse said, in 1939: "I am aware only of the forces I have at my disposal, and I go on, impelled by an idea that I do not fully understand except as it develops during the progress of the picture."

"Thought" is not the same as "idea"; it is the process in the course of which ideas are revealed. And this revelatory process similarly arises out of the relationship between painter and subject. Two other statements made by Matisse are particularly relevant here. The first, recorded in the volume of Matisse's collected writings and statements on art, is a remark made to Tériade in 1929: "My aim is to convey my emotion. This mood is created by the objects around me and which affect me—anything between here and

Chasuble with Green Background
c. 1950

the horizon, down to and including myself. For very often I put myself into the picture, and I am aware of what lies behind me. I express the space and the objects behind me as naturally as if I were looking out over the sea and the sky... I say this only in order to make it clear that the unity realized in my picture, complex though it may be, is not something I find difficult to achieve, indeed it comes quite naturally to me. My sole concern is to convey my emotion...''

I would think that no one before Matisse has suggested so vividly the almost tangible reality of the painter's mental universe—a reality vividly depicted in, for example, *The Pink Studio*, of 1911, and *The Painter and his Model*, of 1917. Emotion, Matisse explains, is created out of the objects around him, and which affect him. An interaction is set up between the painter's environment and his mental world, so that the two become congruent, occupying the same space "between here and the horizon, down to and including myself." Matisse goes on to say: "I put myself into the picture, and I am aware of what lies behind me." In other words, the act of entering the picture takes place within the unified space of the mental vision—a vision that, far from keeping the artist separate him from his surroundings, serves instead to introduce him into a continuity encompassing what lies behind as well as what is in front: for mental space is accessible in all directions at once. The painter can then proceed quite logically to represent that unity of space on the canvas. For the canvas is not intended to represent the model or the object but the painter's vision—a vision that subsumes the functions representer and represented + the purely mental aspects of their representations + the feelings these induce + the overall unity that is thereby created, communicative in its intensity, the whole basis of expressive space.

The other significant statement by Matisse is a note he inserted in the margin of Aragon's manuscript, reproduced by Aragon in *Henri Matisse, roman* (I, 208): "I have for a long time now been conscious of expressing myself through light, or in light, which seems to me like a block of crystal in which something is happening—but it was not until I had enjoyed the light of

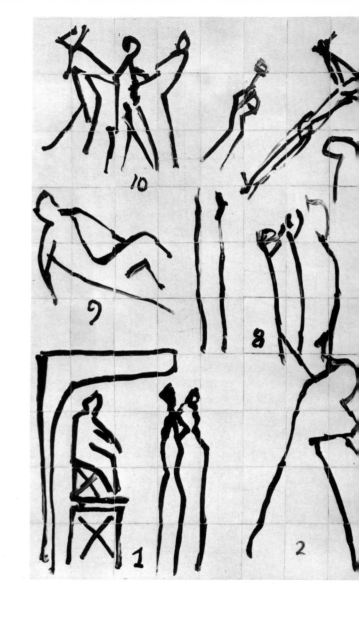

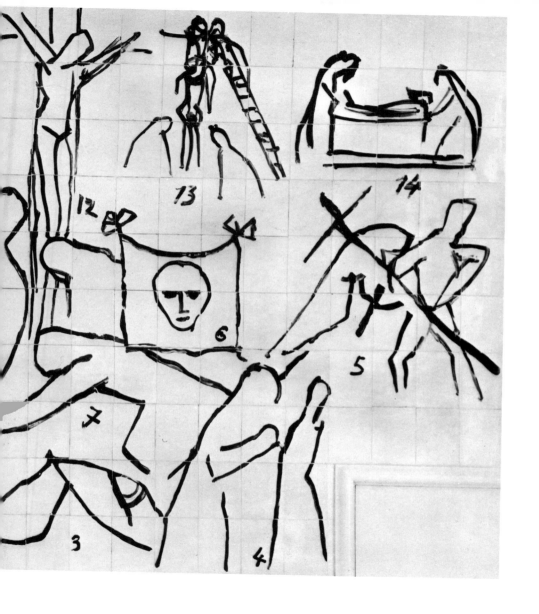

Stations of the Cross
1949-51

day for some long time that I attempted to express myself through the light of the spirit... Fascinated by light, I often reflected, as I escaped in spirit from the restricted space around my motif—such a space, it seems to me, as was considered sufficient by the painters of the past—at all events, I escaped from this space at the back of the motif in the picture and sensed in spirit, beyond myself, beyond any motif, studio, or house even, a cosmic space where one was as little conscious of walls as a fish in the sea... Painting, then, becomes airy; it takes wing. So, as my 'pictorial space' expanded, I often wondered as I worked about the character of the light of the Tropics... To understand our Western light properly you need something to compare it with. When I went to Tahiti I encountered on the way the crystalline light of New York (my first port of call). Also that of the Pacific. The different lights I had experienced made me more determined than ever to imagine the spiritual light I am referring to, born of all the different lights I have absorbed."

Although widely separated in time (1929 and 1942), the two accounts are complementary, and between them they do much to clarify the nature of "pictorial" or "expressive" space. It is, first, a space created out of the painter's mind and its relationship, through the medium of a revelatory subject, with the universe; and it is a space airy with light and made substantial through light. It would be quite wrong to assume that such notions have anything to do with a religious spirituality. On the contrary. All Matisse is trying to do is express, as straightforwardly as possible, feelings he has experienced, and explored, for many years, and for which he has no other vocabulary.

The marginal note in Aragon's manuscript is particularly interesting as an insight into Matisse's intentions regarding the chapel at Vence. In 1952, speaking to Maria Luz about his cutouts, Matisse happened to remark: "From *The Joy of Life*—I was then thirty-five—to this cutout—I am now eighty-two—I have remained the same... because, all this time, I have striven for the same things, perhaps realizing them by different means. My aims were no different when I did the chapel. In a very restricted space, no

Icarus
1943

more than five meters wide, I wanted to inscribe—just as I had done before in pictures fifty centimeters or a meter in width—a spiritual space, that is, a space whose dimensions are not limited even by the existence of the objects represented."

Matisse planned every last detail of the chapel, even down to the vestments. The interior is white, its whiteness undiminished by the three large panels, black line-drawings on white tiles of St. Dominic, the Virgin and Child, and the Stations of the Cross. The interior volume is a space filled with light, which enters from the south and the west via fifteen tall slit windows and two other larger windows. On the stained glass is represented a repeated plant motif in lemon yellow, ultramarine, and bottle green, colors that create soft harmonies on the white walls and flood the space with mauve light.

This light makes space palpable, renders its insubstantiality visible: As the outer walls seem to melt away, so the enclosed volume of air becomes an element suggestive of infinity. Here we see at last "spiritual space" as conceived of by Matisse, infinitely expansive now that it is no longer tied to representation, as it must inevitably be in painting and drawing.

"My chapel," Matisse wrote, "is for me the culmination of a whole lifetime of work, the flowering of a huge effort of honest and difficult endeavor." In the letter offering the chapel as a gift to Monsignor Rémond, Matisse explained: "This piece of work has demanded four years of single-minded and concentrated work, and it is the outcome of the whole of my active life. I regard it as my masterpiece." The space of the chapel makes a living reality out of what, in painting, could only be invoked, by means of sign and illusion, to represent a reality of the mind in terms of ideas. It is a space where "inside" and "outside" are without meaning, no more than lingering memories of walls dissolved now into an infinity where the spirit moves at will, like "a fish in the sea." The "sea" of air and light is essentially the same as that "soothing influence on the mind" dreamed of since 1908, and it is too the elixir of happiness that is the "joy of life." Matisse himself declared: "I

Two Negresses
1908

Large Red Interior
1948

want visitors to the chapel to feel an unburdening of the spirit and, even if they are unbelievers, experience it as a place where the spirit is uplifted, thoughts are made clear, or feeling itself is eased..."

Matisse had long been preoccupied with a desire, first to attain, and then to communicate, just this "unburdening": the chapel at Vence is a monument to a religion that has no god but light itself ("spiritual light... born of all the different lights I had experienced"). A rereading of his collected writings and statements on art serves only to confirm this interpretation—or, rather, it makes it the only possible interpretation, once one understands the meaning that Matisse placed on certain key words such as "feeling," "conception," "whole," "simplification," "space," "light," and "emotion."

"Ease" or "unburdening," for Matisse, were closely related to simplification: and it was through simplification that he liberated form from the isolation it suffered in traditional drawing, with its values, shadows, and modeling, gradually allowing the interior of the form to rise to the surface, free of restriction, airy and untrammeled. In painting he had already achieved this "unburdening" in effecting the transition from descriptive color to expressive color. Form, spatially independent, had become communicative.

Using pure color, with its vibrant juxtapositions, it was almost possible to ignore limitations and separations, but line itself was another matter. Was it not inevitable that line, in drawing, would always separate the internal from the external? By executing line-drawing of the utmost purity, Matisse succeeded in blurring the distinction, miraculously transforming a gesture of enclosure into a gesture of revelation. And yet there must always have been for him an element of dissatisfaction in knowing that he was both a supreme colorist and a supreme draughtsman, and still could not bring the two strands together in the perfect whole he imagined.

In creating the Merion *Dance*, Matisse used for the first time the paper cutouts that enabled him to experiment with full-size forms, but he did not

Hair
1952

immediately capitalize on the newly discovered technique. It was not until 1942 that he made the leap from using cutouts for a purely practical purpose to cutouts used for the purposes of expression, prompted by a commission from Tériade to produce a book of color reproductions similar in style to his covers for the magazine *Verve*. Matisse began work on the project in 1943-44, cutting the motifs he wished to assemble out of sheets of paper painted with gouache. In 1944 he decided on the format of the plates and the title, *Jazz*. In 1946 he decided the plates should be accompanied by pages of text, and began the calligraphic reproduction of the notes comprising the text. In the first of these notes he explained: "My aim here is to show color plates to their greatest advantage. In order to do this I need to separate them by intervals of a quite different character. I judged that handwriting suited my purposes best. That exceptional quality handwriting possesses seemed to me the essential decorative complement to the character of the color plates."

Published on 30 September 1947, *Jazz* consists of twenty plates, fifteen of them double-page spreads. It represents the achievement by Matisse of an entirely new form of expression, resolving finally the contradiction between drawing, which encloses space, and color, which sets it free: Contour is now one with surface, and form is carved directly in space. It can surely be no accident that, at the moment of banishing drawing proper from his work, Matisse should have chosen a handwritten text as the most fitting complement to his color plates—a means of allowing the drawn line to reassert itself in another guise.

First Matisse would prepare his space. This he did by spreading gouache onto a sheet of white paper in such a way as to give a uniform, matt surface, monochrome and unreflective, but nevertheless enlivened and made airy by the traces of brushmarks. Next he would use scissors to cut forms out of the space of the paper sheet. Finally he would assemble the forms into a montage and stick this onto a prepared surface.

On 22 February 1948, Matisse wrote to Rouveyre: "The walls of my room are covered in cutouts." Yet it was not until some years later that Matisse

The Snail
1953

Henri Matisse in Vence
1944-45

Sorrow of the King
1952

exploited his new technique to the full. Most of the period 1946-48 was devoted to painting and Indian ink drawings, which he produced in large numbers; after that, up to 1951, the Vence chapel filled all his waking hours.

The last paintings are among Matisse's finest: *Asia*, 1946; *The Inhabited Silence of Houses*, 1947; and the series of Vence interiors, among them *Yellow and Blue Interior*, 1946, and *Large Red Interior*, 1948. In these canvases space is synthetic in its effect, drawing all the dimensions together into a single plane, a plane that corresponds to a color/light. This latter in an entirely new element, flooding over all the visible objects, revealing each one individually and at the same time establishing a unity between them. Matisse wrote, again to Rouveyre, that the color of the interiors was "invented entirely according to the feeling aroused in me by the presence of nature itself"—in other words, color was the direct physical manifestation of the encounter between the painter's mind and the real world.

While still working on the chapel, Matisse produced one particularly fine cutout, *Zulma*, 1950. With that exception, most of his major cutouts date from 1952: *The Acrobats; Sorrow of the King; The Frog;* the series of *Blue Nudes;* and *Hair*.

If color is space, it is also light, the energy that flows through space. What Matisse calls "feeling" is the electricity of this relationship, capable of transcending boundaries and penetrating matter in such a way that form is opened up and emanates as a kind of presence. When Matisse takes hold of a sheet of paper prepared with gouache, all that he holds in his hands is an ordinary piece of painted paper. But his vision, and the desire for expression that flows from it, at once transform this paper into an object with a density of its own—change it, in fact, into the space he is conscious of within himself and that is now expanding to fill every available area—including even the insignificant surface it needs to inhabit in order to become visible. It is at this moment that the painter's hand slices into the space created about him by his own thought and effort.

Sword Swallower
1943-44

The Sheaf
1953

Something that is itself limitless can become visible only with the help of an object that is limited, but which serves as a revelatory medium. The painter, however, well aware of the operation of his process—which he has exploited to the minutest degree in searching out all the ways in which the object can be made to fulfil its revelatory function—continues to dream of transcending even this limitation. Gradually he begins to transform object into sign, representing the body of the form without its outer skin—for the sign can exist in the internal and the external world, or in both at once, and it can be represented without thereby losing its wider significance.

Thus, when Matisse cuts into the gouache-painted paper, it is actually within himself that he carves the form; there is no line now to hold the form distinct from space, because it is *in* space. Snail or flower, leaf or blue nude, it is a recognizable form that is cut by the scissors, yet its recognizability does not limit it to inhabit the skin of any one particular thing; form is not so much defined as unleashed, one space set within another.

As Matisse carved, he was manipulating space itself, cutting into blocks of color/light, acting directly on the "unity" existing in that second between his own mental space and that of the real world. The way he then proceeded to assemble these spatial forms created something quite new in the history of art, an original art-form that became at once accepted as part of painting, art, and representation itself: the ultimate union of viewer and viewed, thought and reality.

"It is the simplest of means," Matisse had said years before, "that allow the painter to express himself best." Now he said: "What led me to do cutouts was the desire to link color and drawing in a single act." And again: "There is no fundamental split between my earlier pictures and my cutouts. It is just that, with greater purity and greater abstraction, I have achieved a form distilled down to its essentials."

Matisse also said: "Cutting without preliminaries into color reminds me of the direct carving of sculptors." When Matisse himself worked in clay, it was his habit to touch the model; he would then try to convey that sense of touch in his work, rather than suggest a likeness. Touch was thus the means of making volume felt, of evoking the tactile experience and roundedness of a volume of space. It is extraordinary, and moving, to think that at the end of his life, through the cutouts, Matisse found a means of reconciling sight and touch in a single sensation. The fulfillment it brought him is apparent from something he said to André Verdet: "You cannot imagine, in this period of the cutouts, how the sensation of flying that pervades me helps to guide my hand as it controls the path of the scissors. It is rather hard to explain, but I would describe it as a sort of linear equivalent, or graphic, of the sensation of flying. And then too there's the way space becomes vibrant..."

The sensation of flying that pervades me
helps to guide
my hand...
it is a sort of linear equivalent,
or graphic,
of the sensation of flying...
And then too... space becomes vibrant...
The painter need not project himself.
The painter need no longer be the master of illusions:
he takes flight within himself and the surge
carries him beyond his own self.
The world is in his head, or his head *is* the world.
Everywhere the same light. The same air.

"As I create these colored cutouts, it seems to me that I advance joyfully to meet whatever awaits. I do not believe I have ever experienced such peace and harmony as in making these cutout papers. But I know it will be many years before people understand how much what I am doing today anticipated the future."

BIOGRAPHY

1869
Birth of Henri Matisse in Le Cateau-Cambrésis (Nord) on 31 December, in his grandfather's house; his parents ran a general shop stocking a range of paints, in Bohain-en-Vermandois, a village between Le Cateau and Saint-Quentin. He later confided to Pierre Courthion: "Everything I have done comes from my parents, simple hard-working folk."

1882-87
"Son of a grain merchant, destined to follow in my father's footsteps"—there was nothing to suggest Matisse would become a painter. Because of poor health, encouraged to pursue his education; specialized in Latin and Greek at the Lycée Henri-Martin in Saint-Quentin.

1887-88
After two years studying Law in Paris—having first considered a course in Pharmacy—qualified as a lawyer's clerk. Left Paris, "never once having thought of visiting any of the museums, not even the annual painting Salon."

1889
Appointed clerk to the lawyer Derriau, in Saint-Quentin. At the same time attended drawing classes at the Ecole Quentin-de-La-Tour. Told François Coupeaux, in 1947: "I spent several years suffocated with boredom, wanting only to paint before I went to the office at nine o'clock... After the day's work (at six o'clock in the evening) I returned as fast as I could to my room to paint until nightfall."

1890
Given an artist's kit by his mother when convalescing from appendicitis. Copied colored reproductions to pass the time.

1891
In spite of opposition from his father, returned to Paris and enrolled at the Académie Julian, in the studio run by William Bouguereau and Gabriel Ferrier. Entered by Bouguereau for the competititive entrance examination held by the Ecole des Beaux-Arts. Failed to gain a place in February 1892.

1892
At the Ecole des Arts Décoratifs met Albert Marquet, who became—and was to remain—his closest friend.

1895
Formally enrolled in Gustave Moreau's studio, at the Beaux-Arts, where fellow-students included Rouault, Evenepoël, Bussy, Desvallières, Flandrin, and Camoin. Copied the old masters, notably at the Louvre. Lived at 19, quai Saint-Michel. Spent the summer traveling in Brittany, with Albert Wéry.

1896
At the annual Salon of the Société Nationale des Beaux-Arts exhibited two still-lifes, one a *Woman Reading*, purchased by the state, the other a *Studio Interior*; both attracted favorable comment. Nominated by Puvis de Chavannes, and successfully elected, as an associate member of the Salon. In

1897, took advantage of his rights as a member to submit five canvases, one being *The Dinner Table*, which was sharply criticized. Moreau defended him. In the summer, went again to Brittany, where he practiced *plein air* painting for the first time. Color and sunlight became significant elements in his work.

1898

Married Amélie-Noémie-Alexandrine Parayre. Went to London, on Pissarro's advice (to see the Turners), then traveled in Corsica and the South of France. Death of Gustave Moreau.

1899

Returned to the Ecole des Beaux-Arts, where Cormon had replaced Moreau. Following disagreements, left Cormon's studio, together with Marquet and Camoin. Attended life-drawing classes at the Académie Julian. Also worked at the Académie Carillo, rue du Vieux-Colombier, where Eugene Carrière was a tutor. From eight until ten in the evening attended sculpture classes at the Ecole d'Art Municipale in the rue Etienne-Marcel. Now a regular visitor at the *avant-garde* galleries, particularly that run by Ambroise Vollard, from whom he purchased a van Gogh drawing, a Rodin plastercast, a head of a boy by Gauguin, and Cézanne's *Three Bathers*, presented thirty-seven years later to the Musée du Petit-Palais. "Having owned it for thirty-seven years, I know this canvas quite well, although

Le Faune, 1932

Figure with Fish Bowl, 1929

not completely, I hope; it gave me mental sustenance in the difficult moments of my career as an artist; I drew from it my faith and perseverance."

1900

To support the expenses of married life, worked with Marquet on friezes for the Grand-Palais, then being constructed as part of the preparations for the World, Fair. Fell ill, and went to the Alps to recuperate. Painted very little ("I don't think mountain landscapes are of much use to painters. The difference in scale inhibits intimate contact.")

1901

Exhibited at the Salon des Indépendants.

1902

First exhibition at the Berthe Weill gallery. Severe depression due to financial worries. Considered abandoning painting as a career. Spent the winter near Bohain.

1903

Exhibited at the Salon d'Automne, enthusiasm restored.

1904

Exhibition of 46 canvases at Vollard's gallery (catalogue preface by Roger Marx). Spent the summer in Saint-Tropez with Signac, who introduced him to Félix Fénéon.

1905

A stormy reception at the Salon d'Automne for *Woman with the Hat*, which was however bought by Michael and Sarah Stein. It was a turning point in his life: thereafter his pictures found buyers, financial worries were over, and success was assured.

1906

One-man-show at the Druet gallery (55 canvases). Submitted a single major canvas to the Salon des Indépendants, *The Joy of Life*, purchased by Leo Stein.

1907

Apollinaire wrote a laudatory article in *La Phalange:* "When I came toward you, Matisse, the crowds looked at you, and as they laughed you smiled. People saw a monster where was a miracle... Henri Matisse creates a fabric of ideas, he constructs his pictures with colors and lines in a way that brings his combinations to life, that makes them seem exactly right, so that they form a finished composition from which it would be impossible to remove a single color or line without reducing the whole to a haphazard assembly of a few lines and colors. Bringing order to chaos, that is creation. And if an artist's goal is to create, order must be governed by intuition."

1908

Persuaded by Sarah Stein and Hans Purrmann to found an "academy," destined to last no more than a few years. "It demanded a lot of my energy. So I thought: should I be a teacher or a painter? And I closed down the studio." With the good offices of Félix Fénéon, negotiated his first contract with the

Bernheim gallery. The Russian collector Shchukin commissioned *La Danse* and *La Musique*.

1909
Exhibition in Moscow. Bought a house in Issy-les-Moulineaux. "I live ten minutes by railway (54 trains a day) from the Gare Montparnasse."

1910
Retrospective at the Bernheim-Jeune gallery, organized by Félix Fénéon. Trip to Spain.

1911
Trip to Moscow.

1912
First exhibition of sculpture, in London. Visit to Morocco. From Tangier, wrote to Camoin: "We are enjoying the fine weather and the vegetation, which is absolutely luxuriant. I have done some work, and I'm not too unhappy with it, although it is difficult; the light is so soft, it's quite different from the mediterranean."

1913
Exhibition "Tableaux du Maroc et sculptures" at the Bernheim-Jeune gallery. Contributed to the international exhibition that launched modern art in the United States, the Armory Show (New York, Chicago, Boston).

1914
In Paris at the outbreak of war. Spent the summer in Collioure.

1915
Exhibition in New York.

Sleeping Woman, 1949

La Belle Tahitienne, 1937

1916

Began to spend more time in Nice (at the Hôtel Beaurivage).

1918

Visited Renoir in Cagnes. Exhibition with Picasso at the Paul Guillaume gallery. "If I didn't do what I do, I should like to paint like Picasso," he confided to Max Jacob—only to receive the reply: "Well, that's strange! Do you know, Picasso said the same thing to me about you."

1920

Executed maquettes of the sets and costumes for the ballet *Le Rossignol* (music by Stravinsky, choreography by Massine), in a production by Diaghilev's Ballets Russes company.

1922

Exhibition at the Bernheim-Jeune gallery (and regularly thereafter until 1927).

1924

Exhibition in Copenhagen.

1926

Trip to Italy (Naples and Sicily).

1927

Exhibition in New York.

1928

Exhibitions in London and at the Valentine Gallery, New York.

1930

Trip Tahiti, via New York—where he considered living permanently—and San Francisco. "The time in Tahiti was very fruitful. I had a strong urge to experience for myself the light on the far side of the Equator, to establish contact with the trees there, get inside things.

Every light has a particular harmony. It creates an entirely different atmosphere. The light of the Pacific, the South Sea islands, is like looking deep into a goblet of gold. I remember at first, when I arrived, it was disappointing, and then, bit by bit, it was beautiful, beautiful... it is beautiful!"

1931

Illustrated Mallarmé's *Poems* for Skira. "Etchings with a fine, regular line, no cross-hatching, leaving the printed sheet almost as white as before. The drawing fills the unbordered page, so that the paper appears even lighter, for the drawing is not concentrated toward the center, as it usually is, but spreads out over the whole sheet."

1932

Worked on the *Dance* commissioned by Albert C. Barnes, an enthusiastic collector of his paintings. "I had had the idea for a long time and had already used it in *The Joy of Life*, and then in my first large composition... For a period of three years I had to keep reinterpreting my work, like a film director. When I am working it really is like continually shooting a film. But with this piece, I was conditioned just as much by the architecture, for that was the principal consideration."

1933

Went for a course of treatment to Abano, near Venice. Every day traveled to Padua to see Giotto's frescoes. "For me Giotto is the summit of my ambitions, but the path that leads to something equivalent in our day and age is too difficult and long to be accomplished within a single lifetime," Matisse wrote to Bonnard in 1946.

1934

Exhibition at the gallery recently opened by his son, Pierre Matisse, in New York.

1936

Exhibitions in London, Paris and San Francisco (paintings, drawings, and sculpture).

1938

Moved to Cimiez, in the hills above Nice, occupying an apartment in the former Hôtel Regina. Executed maquettes of the sets and costumes for the ballet *Rouge et Noir* (music by Shostakovich, choreography by Massine).

1941

Had major abdominal surgery, from which he made a full recovery.

1943

Moved to the villa "Le Rêve" (Vence), where he lived until 1949, before moving back to the Regina. Major retrospective of his paintings (1898-1938) at Pierre Matisse's gallery in New York.

1944

Embarked on a series of gouaches and pasted paper cutouts, later collected in a book entitled *Jazz*, published by Tériade in 1947.

1945

Exhibited with Picasso at the Victoria and Albert Museum, London (catalogue

White Mask, 1951

with preface by Christian Zervos). Disliked Surrealism ("I have just received the illustrated catalogue of the Surrealist exhibition at the Maeght gallery, and I was repelled by the overwrought detail of these imaginings," he wrote to André Rouveyre on 22 July 1947); but was interested in Soutine—he asked his son to buy one of his pictures at public auction—and also, in the postwar years, in Dubuffet, who reminded him of Soutine, "although more delicate."

1946
Illustrated *Lettres d'une religieuse portugaise* (Tériade) and *Visages* by Pierre Reverdy (Editions du Chêne).

1947
Exhibition in Liège.

1948
Traveling exhibition of his drawings, organized by The American Federation of Arts (Philadelphia, Beverly Hills, San Francisco, Minneapolis, Chicago, Washington, Baltimore, etc.) Worked on the building and decoration of the Chapel of the Rosary at Vence. "I see the need to free myself from all constraints, all theoretical preconceptions, in order to express the depths of my being, placing myself outside time, beyond the distinction between the figurative and the nonfigurative," he wrote in December 1947 to Rouveyre. To Picasso, who reproached him for working on a church and suggested he try a market instead,

he retorted: "I don't give a damn: I have greens greener than pears and oranges more orange than pumpkins. So why should I care?"

1949
Exhibition of recent work (1947-49) at the Musée d'Art moderne de la Ville de Paris (catalogue with foreword by Jean Cassou).

1950
Exhibition at the Galerie des Ponchettes (Nice) and the Maison de la Pensée Française in Paris (catalogue with preface by Aragon).
Major exhibition in Milan.

1951
Exhibition in Japan (Tokyo, Kyoto, Osaka). Exhibition "Le Fauvisme" at the Musée d'Art moderne de la Ville de Paris.

1952
Exhausted by the major undertakings of the last years (the chapel and the paper cutouts), unable to work as much as he would have liked. "All my organs are sound," he wrote to Father Couturier. "Only my batteries are flat. Yet my potential for creativity is still there, intact..." Opening of the Musée Matisse in Le Cateau-Cambrésis.

1954
Death of Matisse on 3 November, following a heart attack.

BIBLIOGRAPHY

Matisse's various statements and writings on art have been collected together by Dominique Fourcade under the title *Ecrits et propos sur l'art* ("Savoir" series, Hermann, 1972). English translations were collected and edited by Jack D. Flam, *Matisse on Art* (Phaidon, London and New York, 1973). A particularly interesting exchange of letters between Matisse and Camoin appears under the title "Correspondance Matisse-Camoin," in issue 12 of *La Revue de l'Art* (1971); and Jean Clair has published in *La Nouvelle Revue Française* (nos. 211 and 212, Gallimard, 1970) a "Correspondance Matisse-Bonnard (1925-1946)."

Matisse's *œuvre* has inspired numerous articles, critical studies, and monographs, but there are a number of publications which, in their different ways, seem to be particularly useful accounts of the artist and his work. Indispensable is the comprehensive study by Alfred H. Barr, Jr., *H. Matisse: His Art and His Public* (Museum of Modern Art Series, New York, 1951). Another invaluable source is Louis Aragon's book *Henri Matisse, roman* (2 vols., Gallimard, Paris, 1971; translated as *Henri Matisse: A Novel* Collins, London, and Harcourt Brace Jovanovich, New York, 1972). There are also informative monographs by Jean-Louis Ferrier (*Matisse, 1911-1930;* Hazan, Paris, 1961) and Raymond Escholier (*Matisse, ce vivant;* Fayard, Paris, 1956; translated as *Matisse: A Portrait of the Artist and the Man*, Faber & Faber, London, and Praeger, New York, 1960). And, finally, Pierre Schneider's masterly and perceptive work has already proved its worth (*Matisse*; Flammarion, Paris, 1984; translated as *Matisse*, Thames and Hudson; London and New York, 1984). Of particular interest with regard to the cutouts is Jean Guichard-Meili's *Matisse, les Gouaches découpées* (Hazan, Paris, 1983; translated as *Matisse Paper Cutouts*, Thames and Hudson, London and New York, 1984).

Mention must also be made of the recently inaugurated series of *Cahiers Henri Matisse*, launched to coincide with the refurbishment of the Musée Matisse in Nice: these publications are intended to complement exhibitions held at the Museum, and to act as a forum for discussion of Matisse's work and influence. Titles published in 1986 cover the themes: Matisse and Tahiti; Matisse's photographs; and Matisse's book-illustrations.

LIST OF ILLUSTRATIONS

57 : *Seated Nude (Nu assis)*, 1930, drypoint.

59 : *The Dream (Le Rêve)*, 1935, oils on canvas, 80 × 65 cm. Musée national d'Art moderne, Paris.

60 : *Woman with Blouse, Dreaming (Femme à la blouse, rêvant)*, 1936, pen-and-ink drawing.

61 : *The Romanian Blouse (La Blouse roumaine)*, 1940, oils on canvas, 92 ×73 cm. Musée national d'Art moderne, Paris.

64 : *Woman Reading, Black Background (Liseuse sur fond noir)*, 1939, oils on canvas, 92 × 73.5 cm. Musée national d'Art moderne, Paris.

65 : *Woman on a Sofa (Femme au divan)*, 1920-22, oils on canvas, 60 × 73.5 cm. Doetsch-Benziger Bequest, Kunstmuseum, Basel.

66 : *The Egyptian Curtain (Le Rideau égyptien)*, 1948, oils on canvas, 116.2 × 88.9 cm. Phillips Collection, Washington.

67 : *The Persian Robe (La Robe persane)*, 1937. Private collection.

69 : *Dancer and Armchair, Black Background (Danseuse, fond noir, fauteuil rocaille)*, 1942. A. Matisse Collection, Lebanon, Connecticut.

71 : *Hélène*, 1936, oils on canvas, 50 × 30 cm.

72 : *The Inhabited Silence of Houses (Le Silence habité des maisons)*, 1947, oils on canvas, 61 × 50 cm. Private collection, Paris.

73 : *Yellow and Blue Interior (Intérieur jaune et bleu)*, 1946, oils on canvas, 116×81 cm. Musée national d'Art moderne, Paris.

74 : *Primavera*, 1938, engraving, 226 ×168 cm. *(Photo: Roger-Viollet)*.

76 : *Chasuble with Green Background (Chasuble à fond vert)*, c. 1950, gouache on paper cutout. Musée Matisse, Nice. *(Photo: Maurice Bérard, Nice.)*

78/79 : *Stations of the Cross (Chemin de croix)*, painted and enameled ceramic, 348 × 530 cm. Dominican Chapel of the Rosary, Vence. *(Photo: Hélène Adant.)*

81 : *Icarus (Icare)*, 1943, gouache on paper cutout, illustration for *Jazz*, Tériade, Paris, 1947. *(Photo: Claude Caroly, Paris.)*

83 : *Two Negresses (Les Deux Négresses)*, 1908, bronze. Museum of Art, Baltimore.

84 : *Large Red Interior (Grand Intérieur rouge)*, 1948, oils on canvas, 146 × 97 cm. Musée national d'Art moderne, Paris.

86 : *Asia (Asie)*, 1946, oils on canvas, 116 ×81 cm. Mrs. Mollie Parnis Livingston Collection, New York.

87 : *Hair (La Chevelure)*, 1952, lithograph after gouache on paper cutout, *Verve*, Tériade, Paris, 1958.

89 : *The Snail (L'Escargot)*, 1953, lithograph after gouache on paper cutout, *Verve*, Tériade, Paris, 1958.

90/91 : Henri Matisse in Vence, 1944-45. *(Photo: Henri Cartier-Bresson.)*

92 : *Sorrow of the King (Tristesse du roi)*, 1952, lithograph after gouache on paper cutout, *Verve*, Tériade, Paris, 1958.

94 : *Sword Swallower (L'Avaleur de sabres)*, 1943-44, gouache on paper cutout, illustration for *Jazz*, Tériade, Paris, 1947. *(Photo: Claude Caroly, Paris.)*

95 : *The Sheaf (La Gerbe)*, 1953, lithograph after gouache on paper cutout, *Verve*, Tériade, Paris, 1958.

97 : top: *Nude, half-face (Nu au visage coupé)*, 1914, lithograph. Bibliothèque nationale, Paris.
bottom: *Reclining Figure, head on hand (Figure allongée, tête dans la main)*, 1929, engraving. Bibliothèque nationale, Paris.

99 : top: *Le Faune*, illustration for Stéphane Mallarmé's *Poems*, 1932. Bibliothèque nationale, Paris.
bottom: *Figure with Fish Bowl (Figure face au bocal à poissons)*, 1929, etching. Bibliothèque nationale, Paris.

101 : top: *Sleeping Woman (Femme endormie)*, 1949. Musée des Beaux-Arts, Besançon.
bottom: *La Belle Tahitienne*, 1937.

103 : *White Mask (Masque blanc)*, 1951, aquatint.
Bibliothèque nationale, Paris.

Cover illustrations: *Apples (Les Pommes)*, oils on canvas, 116.8 × 89.4 cm. The Art Institute of Chicago.